A Comparative Study On Metro Manila's Train Lines And Commuter Satisfaction

A research presented to the

Humanities and Social Sciences Strand

Senior High School

Ateneo De Manila University

In partial fulfilment of the requirements

for the

Quantitative Research class

Luis Andres Augusto P. Amatong

Marianne Denise J. Bayucan

Marco Angelo G. Francisco

Mikka Alexis T. Mendoza

Janelle Fiona M. Torres

March 2019

Acknowledgements

We, the researchers, would like to give thanks to our adviser, Ma'am Reyjane Calicdan, who guided us throughout the duration of our research. We are very grateful for all the advice you have given which helped in the completion of our study. Apart from that, we would also like to thank you for your undying patience as well as your efforts to motivate us in completing our research despite the unforeseen difficulties we have encountered.

We would then like to thank our panelists and classmates from the class 11-Mayer for giving us critique and comments which helped us improve our research. Without these comments, the research may not even have reached five chapters.

Table of Contents

Acknowledgements ii

Table of Figures vi

Abstract viii

Chapter 1 Introduction 9

Background of the Study 9

Statement of the Problem 10

Objectives 11

Significance of the Study 12

Scope and Limitations 13

Chapter 2 15

Review of Related Literature and Studies 15

History of Rail Transit Systems in the Philippines 15

Studies on Train Systems 18

Studies on Other Types of Transport Systems 20

Conceptual Framework 28

Hypothesis 30

Definition of Terms 30

Operational Framework 31

Synthesis 33

Chapter 3 34

Methodology 34

Research Design 34

Variables and Measure 35

Research Participants 36

Sampling 37

Instruments 37

Procedures for Data Gathering 40

Procedures for Data Analysis 40

Chapter 4 42

Analysis and Interpretation of Data 42

Results from Preliminary Questions 42

Results from Demographic Data 44

Results from the Main Questionnaire 45

Survey Anova results 47

Chapter 5 50

Summary, Conclusions, and Recommendations   50

    Findings   51

    Conclusions   51

    Recommendations   52

References   62

Curriculum Vitae   66

    Mikka Alexis Mendoza   66

    Janelle Torres   70

    Luis Amatong   74

    Denise Bayucan   76

    Marco Francisco   78

Table of Figures

Figure 1. Dimensions of customer satisfaction scale 22

Figure 2. Level of functionality scale 23

Figure 3. Graph of four categories of features 24

Figure 4. KANO Evaluation Table 25

Figure 5. The study of correlation among the factors: railway transit systems, commuter's

satisfaction, and commuting time. 27

Figure 6. Chronbach's Alpha Formula 37

Figure 7. Chronbach's Alpha for Time component of the survey. 38

Figure 8. Chronbach's Alpha for the Comfort component of the survey. 38

Figure 9. Chronbach's Alpha for the Reliability component of the survey. 38

Figure 10. Chronbach's Alpha for the Security component of the survey. 39

Figure 11. Survey's Chronbach's Alpha taken from the mean of all four components 39

Figure 12. Percentage of respondents using each train line. 41

Figure 13. Number of breakdowns the respondents experienced. 42

Figure 14. Age Demographic. 43

Figure 15. Result to the item that states "I would like it if my time spent commuting could

be lessened". 44

Figure 16. Neutral result in the item "I dislike taking the MRT/LRT because of how

unreliable it can be." 45

Figure 17. Result to the item, "I would prefer it if the train had air-conditioning / the train's air-conditioning was working."   46

Figure 18. Anova result of individual item "I feel that the trains on the MRT or LRT are too slow."   47

Figure 19. Anova Result of the whole survey for the significance of the train line on the satisfaction of the customer.   48

Figure 20. Anova Result of the whole survey for the significance of the commuting time on the satisfaction of the customer   49

Abstract

This study's objective was to determine the relationship between the different train lines that operate within Metro Manila and commuter's satisfaction. The KANO model was used as the main framework of the research. The premise of the theory is that the satisfaction of a customer is dependent on the Level of Functionality that a product provides.

The data presented was obtained through disseminating a survey from January to March of 2019. 45 respondents were obtained through systematic sampling which did not meet the quota of 60 respondents, deeming the sample too small to make a generalization of the whole population.

The researchers have recommended a larger sample size to accommodate the large population of Metro Manila. In addition, different factors may be considered such as the time of commuting etc. as they were not focused in this research paper.

Chapter 1

Introduction

Background of the Study

Public transport is an integral part of modern society. It is through cost-efficient public transport that we are able to mobilize our workforce and enable them to be efficient workers. In developed countries all around the world, a defining characteristic of their most productive cities is an organized and efficient public transport system. For instance, Japanese commuter trains are upheld to a high standard of quality; to the Japanese, trains are considered running late if they are even a minute behind schedule (Mito, 2018). Likewise, countries like Hong Kong, Singapore, and highly urban cities like London all feature efficient and well planned public transport systems and often rank highly amongst metro systems (Falzon, 2017). According to Schmöcker, Bell, and Lam (2004), efficient public transport is necessary to solve the need for mass transit in highly urbanized cities. They use cheaper public transport to "[incentivize] citizens to leave the car home," likely in order to minimize traffic in these densely populated areas.

One of the many forms of transportation that can be found in the Philippines is the rail transit system. This study will focus on the Metro Rail Transit system (hereafter referred to as MRT) and the Light Rail Transit system (hereafter referred to as LRT). These are found in Metro Manila, and connect many different cities together to facilitate easy transport between the different hubs of commerce. The LRT-1 line is 18.073 kilometers long, connecting Baclaran to Roosevelt, while the LRT-2 line is roughly 12.5 kilometers long, connecting Recto to Santolan. Meanwhile, the MRT-3 is 16.9 kilometers long, connecting North Avenue to Taft Avenue. Both lines suffer serious issues; harassment and frequent breakdowns are common. Cases of PWD harassment (Orellana, 2018), sexual harassment, and gender discrimination (Ramirez, 2018) occur on the trains, alongside near-daily breakdowns. There are even occasions where passengers end up walking the tracks in order to get to their destination (Rey, 2018).

According to Cantwell, Caulfield, and O'Mahony (2007), inefficient or low-quality transport systems, like poor bus or train systems, cause immense amounts of stress. This stress can factor into other processes, like workplace productivity or mental health. Their study done on public transport in Dublin showed strong correlations between densely packed trains full of people and the stress it causes for its users. This correlation is even more important given the role that mass transit plays. Compare the situation of the MRT to the situation of London's Metro system - the efficiency of their system leads to incredibly high satisfaction rates compared to other rail systems internationally, as expected of a country that depends heavily on its train systems. So heavily, in fact, that public advocacies to further improve their systems, like Britain Runs on Rail, have been implemented by the government (Palacin, 2018). If low efficiency results in low workplace productivity and deteriorating mental health, improving the efficiency of objectively poor quality transport systems such as the Philippine MRT-3 line will at the very least neutralize these harms. Thus, it is urgent to be able to define what constitutes an efficient transport system and what factors impact satisfaction and efficiency in order to minimize such risk.

Statement of the Problem

According to an article posted by Michael Bueza on Rappler, in the year 2017, there have been 516 recorded MRT Line 3 problems from the first of January to the 31st of December. In addition to this, the data also stated that the frequency of the occurring problems vary depending on the hour, day, month, and station. With that being said, many commuters still opt to ride the MRT despite these problems, though their satisfaction regarding the said mode of transportation could very well change. It is for this reason that the main research problem formulated is: To what extent is commuters' satisfaction affected by the quality of the railway systems in Metro Manila?

Sub-Questions:

1. What is the demographic of the commuters?

2. How frequent do the commuters commute using the train?

3. Does the commuter's satisfaction factor in their perceived productivity?

4. What is the effect of the experience of commuting on the perceived productivity of the commuter at work/school?

Objectives

This topic will hopefully guide and inform everyone of what is happening in Metro Manila's rail transit systems. This awareness can help influence those who hold a high position in running the rail transit systems, such as the LRT and MRT, to adjust the respective systems accordingly. The researchers aim to do the following in this study:

- to determine the satisfaction of the commuters in the rail lines LRT 1, LRT 2, and MRT 3;

- to identify and categorize the external factors affecting the service quality in the rail networks;

- to analyze how external factors affect the satisfaction of the commuters;

- and to compare which of the three rail lines (namely the LRT 1, LRT 2, and MRT 3) has the least satisfaction and why it is such;

Significance of the Study

The findings of this study will be beneficial to the following:

Filipino Commuters. For those who ride the rail transit system often and for those who ride the trains less frequently, the study will be a helpful guide to how the train system can satisfy its passengers' needs. They will also be able to see what the main cause of dissatisfaction is for those who do ride the train lines often. This will be useful especially for those who are planning to ride the train while hurrying. They might either be encouraged or discouraged to ride the system as they know the situations of others and as they consider whether the rail transit system had been able to satisfy their commuting needs during those times.

Philippine Government. The government will be able to see how satisfied the public is with the performance of the rail transit system and find out what the causes of their satisfaction or dissatisfaction may be. Knowing these factors may help the authorities in charge of the rail transit system improve the train system accordingly.

Institutions. The study will also benefit institutions, like schools and hospitals. Specifically, it will benefit institutions located near train stations, like FEU Manila, San Beda University, and University of Santo Tomas. In their scenario, while there is a prevalence of students who use private cars or buses and other modes of transportation, one of the primary means of transportation students in these schools use is the train. As such, one of the biggest impacts this study will have is on commuters who work in institutions similarly located around the train stations, as they use the train systems as their primary mode of transportation to and from their occupation. We think that a distinction must be made between this group of commuters and other normal users of the train as the the impact of any changes on the train systems (underlying effects such as increases in productivity, for example) will be felt greatest by members of these institutions.

Scope and Limitations

In the Philippines, the rail transit system is composed of four running railway systems, namely: LRT Lines 1 and 2, MRT Line 3, and the Philippine National Railways (PNR) Metro Commuter Line. For the purposes of this research paper, only LRT Lines 1 and 2, and MRT Line 3 will be focused on. These three railway systems are situated around the area of Metro Manila only, unlike PNR which links Metro Manila and Laguna together. Majority of the research paper will focus on Metro Manila-specific commuting problems, which is why the research will not dwell on the PNR for the rest of the paper. It was stated in the background of the study that urbanized areas require efficient public transport to resolve the problem of mass transit

(Schmöcker et al., 2004). Metro Manila is one of the most urbanized areas that have difficulty in organizing efficient public transport. This paper aims to help with that complication, hence the focus only within Metro Manila.

The scope of the research will encompass the aspects of: commuting time on the train only; the satisfaction of the commuter regarding the comfort of usage of the facilities of the train; and the comparison of satisfaction rates among the railway systems: LRT Line 1, LRT Line 2, and MRT Line 3. Certain aspects of the topic will not be considered in the paper, such as the percentage of the commuters that take multiple forms of commuting, the percentage of the commuters that may prefer riding other modes of transportation over the rail transit systems, as well as the percentage of the commuters who take the rail transit systems without the purpose of going to work or school.

The research paper was conducted for about three months, around December 2018 to March 2019, which was dependent on the allotted time given to the researchers for data gathering.

Chapter 2

Review of Related Literature and Studies

This chapter introduced related literature of the researchers' study. The scope of the related literature focused mainly on rail transit systems around the world, which the researchers applied to the Philippines' context of using the LRT 1, LRT 2, and MRT 3 as they are the main rail systems that get people around Metro Manila within the cities of its parameters.

The researchers delved into studies related to the positive aspects of rail transit systems by taking into account the various research papers that were accessed from different contexts and locations around the world. In addition to that, the negative aspects were also looked at for a better view of the pros and cons of the train systems all around the world. The researchers saw how train systems can impact countries around the world whether positively or negatively through this literature review. After condensing all these, the researchers applied the studies to Metro Manila's own context with its rail transit systems: LRT 1, LRT 2, and MRT 3.

The frameworks were taken from all the review of literature, which guided the paper accordingly as the backbone of this research. These explained how the data and results were then analyzed.

History of Rail Transit Systems in the Philippines

The idea of railroads in the Philippines first came about during the time of the Spanish in 1870. By August 6, 1875, there had been a royal order approving to construct and operate railways in the Philippines. Eduardo Lopez Navarro, an engineer of the department of public works, first proposed plans for the railways in 1876 which was submitted to Spain. The plans were suspended until 1883 where a royal decree was published announcing the railway lines in accordance with Navarro's plans. The lines were as follows:

Lines of the North:

From Manila to Dagupan by way of Tarlac

From Dagupan to Laoag by way of the coast

From San Fernando to Iba by way of Subic

From Bigaa to Tuguegarao by way of Baliuag and Cabanatuan

Lines of the South:

From Manila to Taal by way of Calamba, to Albay by way of Santa Cruz and Nueva Caceres

Navarro classified the railway lines in two categories. First were lines that would immediately be profitable commercially. Included in this category were the Manila-Dagupan, Manila-Taal, and Calamba-Santa Cruz lines. The second category were the lines which would bring in profit that was barely enough to cover expenses. In this category were the Dagupan-Laoag, Santa Cruz-Albay, San Fernando-Iba, and Cabanatuan-Tuguegarao lines. However, the construction of the lines faced some problems. However, in the American occupation, the importance of having a public transport system in the form of railroads as recognised. They also recognised that guarantee and encouragement from the government were needed to fulfil the task of construction of the railroads (McIntyre, 1907).

In today's times, the Philippines currently only has three rail transit lines running through Metro Manila: LRT 1, LRT 2, and MRT 3. The president, Ferdinand Marcos, created the government agency Light Rail Transit System Authority (LRTA) on July 12, 1980. The first chairman was the then first lady Imelda Marcos. In October 1981, construction of the train line started and the government appointed the help of Electrowatt Engineering Services of Zurich to manage the project. In 1997, the Manila Metro Rail Transit System Line 3 (MRT 3) started its construction which finished and opened 2 years later in 1999 where the original stations are from North Avenue to Buendia. The remaining section of Buendia to Taft was open to the public the following year. In 2003, phase one of which is from Santolan to Cubao station opened of the LRT 2 line. The remaining stations of the second phase from Betty-Go Belmonte to Legarda was opened a year later. The last station of Reto began its operation the same year of 2004 only 5 months later. The LRT 1 stations of Monumento to Balintawak were opened while the Balintawak to Roosevelt was opened later on of the same year of 2010. The year of 2011 saw an overhaul in the entrance system of the trains where they shifted from a token-based system or a system where a person was given a token to enter the platform area into a ticket-based system where a person taps the ticket in a turnstyle in order to enter the platform area. The next year, the National Economic Development Authority approved extensions of the lines of LRT 1 from Balintawak to Bacoor, Cavite and LRT 2 from Marikina to Masinag. In 2013, the Department of Travel and Communications (DOTC) opened bidding to add carriages to the MRT 3 line in order to decongest the trains especially during rush hour where the demand for the train system is high.

In about 20 years, extension of the system comprised of 150 kilometres of routes (LRTA, n.d. ; Orosa, 2013).

As of 2018, the LRTA has 5 projects for the LRT, 3 of which are locally funded and two foreign assisted. The first locally funded project is the rehabilitation of the units. In 2018, their completed projects include the acquisition of trainset wheels and replacing the Brake Operating Unit (BOU). Some of their on-going implementations as of 2018 are the replacement of rolling stock air-conditioning units and the rehabilitation of the Fire Detection and Alarm System and Fire Suppression System (FDAS). They are also planning on extending the LRT line 2 west. They plan on adding three new stations: a Tutuban station located next to the Custer Mall, a Divisoria station located west of Recto avenue, and a Pier 4 station located north of Zaragosa street. The third plan is a project on the Cubao Interchange. They plan on constructing a passenger walkway from LRT 2 and MRT 3. As for their 2 foreign assisted projects, both projects are extensions for the existing train lines. The first means to extend the LRT Line 1 south making the line traverse through Paranaque and Las Pinas from Baclaran to reach the city of Bacoor. The second means to extend LRT Line 2 from Santolan Station to a proposed Emerald station located in front of Robinson's Metro East and Sta. Lucia Cainta and then to a Masinag Station. The objectives of the extensions of the train lines are to provide safe and reliable transit through Metro Manila and the suburbs. The LRTA also want to alleviate the worsening traffic conditions in the Paranaque-Las Pinas-Cavite area (LRTA, 2018).

Studies on Train Systems

Internationally, railway systems maintain their importance, and there is plenty of research that is conducted in order to improve the efficiency of these railway systems. Extensive research has been conducted, for example, on the feasibility and purpose of light rail systems, (Norley, 2010; Higgins, et. al, 2014) on possible reorganization of European railways, (Profillidis, 2014) or even putting sleeping compartments on commuter trains (Hunter-Zaworski, 2018). International studies have focused mainly on improving existing train systems, by looking at what general factors affect efficiency on railway systems, or other external and context-specific factors could affect efficiency and feasibility of railway systems. Asal Farajpour, et. al, wrote a paper entitled "Identifying the Factors Affecting on Service Quality & Passenger Satisfaction in Commuter Train Services" where they propose the use of two models (SERVQUAL and KANO) to deduce what factors directly or indirectly affect the experience of riding a commuter train. They categorized these factors under five different categories: Empathy, Reliability, Responsiveness, Assurance, and Tangibility. These five categories of factors will be revisited later in the framework of the study. Briefly, however, a summary of each category will be given. Empathy consists of factors such as "employee understanding of passenger needs" or "convenience of commuter train schedules." Reliability consists of factors such as "punctuality of trains" or "ease of station accessibility." Responsiveness pertains to factors such as the "courtesy of the crew" while Assurance pertains to "train safety operations" and "ability of train service staff to answer questions." Finally, Tangibility pertains to the overall quality of the train service as a whole, with factors such as "cleanliness" and "appearance of train personnel."

A study conducted by the Swedish government agency Trafikanalys (Transport Analysis, 2014) claims, "In Sweden, train travel is a common mode of transport and various categories of passenger trains run on the network, all differentiated by their distance, speed, and level of service and comfort... Passenger travel by rail has been increasing over the last few years." In their study, they aimed to compare the railway systems of Japan and Sweden, as both had deregulated their railway systems in the late 1980s, to see the differences between the two. On one hand, Sweden opted for the "vertical separation of operations from the construction, management, and maintenance of infrastructure," meaning different organizations operate different functions of the railway system, while Japan decided to integrate these three areas of operation. Many other differences were drawn between the two systems, however, the study found no answers as to whether or not one system was superior to the other system.

In another study, Shigeru Morichi and Tetsuo Shimizu (2006) discuss possible railway policies that could be plausibly used by other countries. Using Japan's railway system and policies as a basis, the policies of eight different countries ("France, Germany, the United Kingdom, Italy, Spain, Sweden, the United States (US) and Japan") were compared in the study, in order to discuss the pros and the cons of each system and set of policies. One of the conclusions of the study pertained to railway policies for developing countries, where they claim that "the intercity railway (National Railway) problems in developing countries are in the vicious circle with low service level, lack of capacity, limited demand, politically decided fare, low efficiency of operation and lack of investment for infrastructure and rolling stock." These points can be revisited in the study later, as basis for, or used as, factors to be taken into consideration when looking at railway transit efficiency.

Studies on Other Types of Transport Systems

Trains have always been a reliable form of transportation since the 18th century. Though trains have been built and improved upon for over hundreds of years at this point, other forms of transportation are also commonly used by the general population to get to their destinations in their day-to-day life.

Cantwell, Caulfield, & O'Mahony, 2009 stated that the effect of taking the train or a bus can heighten the psycho-physiological functions of a person such as the blood pressure and the neuroendocrine functions which equates to stress while taking these modes of transportation. This means that no matter what type of public transport a person may use, this person is still in risk of increasing their stress levels, simply due to the decision to ride public transportation.

To counter that, Saif, maghrour zefreh, & Torok, 2017 stated that "public transport in urban areas has gained greater attention in recent years for improving sustainability and the quality of urban life". Though it may seem that psychologically speaking, public transport is slowly causing a breakdown upon a person's mental state, it is making good progress in the economic improvement of its surrounding environment. It is an advantage in terms of the area it is in because it provides easy access for the public to travel around.

With that in mind, the following is a list of different forms of public transportation:

Buses and coaches. In the Philippines, riding a bus is typically done for long-distance riding. Its most usual purpose is to carry people from province to province, province to city, or city to province. Specific buses can also provide transportation from city to city within Metro Manila. Coaches, on the other hand, are typically used for a more private purpose for the general public. Instances like checking in a hotel with a shuttle service, hiring a coach bus for provincial trips, and having free shuttle service in several establishments like malls and schools.

Taxis. Before the prevalence of ride-sharing applications like Uber and Grab, the presence of metered taxis in the Philippines provided another form of transportation. Considered more private compared to the previous two, using metered taxis for transportation usually meant that only one rider or one group of riders automatically counted as the taxi's passengers. Carpools were not the usual practice, thus, taking taxi rides is more personal between the driver and his passenger.

Jeepneys. This form of transportation is versatile. Depending on the type of jeepney one person takes, the jeepney can travel from city to city, city to province, province to province, city to subdivision, city to street, province to specific establishments, so on and so forth. Due to the relatively cheap fare compared to the previous forms of transportation, this is what Filipinos use daily to get to their destinations. Sometimes they use multiple jeepneys, one after the other, to be able to travel faster.

Tricycles. This form of transportation usually does short-distance rides. It rides within the district that it is currently in, typically going from street to street, establishment to street, building to house, and house to house. It can carry three to four people, depending on the space allotted inside the cart, which makes the vehicle travel slowly, hence the reason for its short-distance rides.

Theoretical Framework

The KANO model was named after its developer Noriaki Kano back in who is a Japanese researcher and consultant which was published back in 1984. The main premises of the model were: the dependence of customer satisfaction on the Level of Functionality that a product provides; the features of the model can be categorized into four categories; and the means of determining a customer's satisfaction through the use of a questionnaire (Zacarias, n.d.).

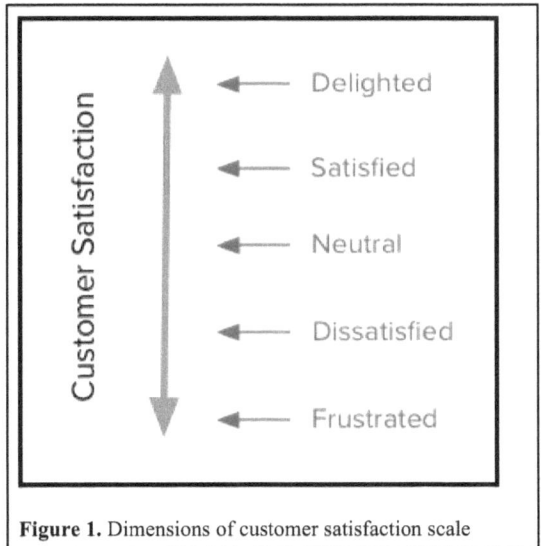

Figure 1. Dimensions of customer satisfaction scale

The model states that there are levels of satisfaction a customer can reach namely the most positive feeling of delighted, then satisfied, neutral, dissatisfied and finally frustrated. In Figure 1, it is vital to point out that the scale is rather not linear.

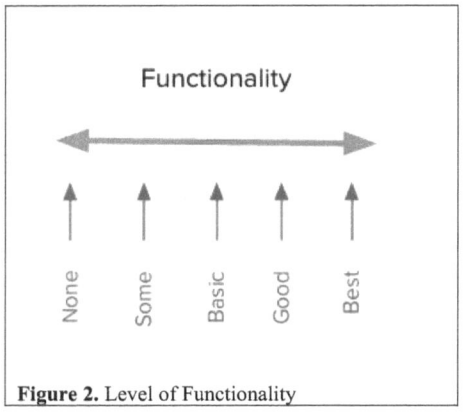

Figure 2. Level of Functionality

Figure 2, on the other hand shows how an object's functionality is rated from Best to None. This represents an investment wherein it features how much value a customer gets from a product. It is an investment because it shows how much a customer "invests" in a product once he or she has bought it. In conclusion, these two dimensions combined can create a basis of the KANO model to detect whether or not a customer is satisfied or not with the product (Zacarias, n.d.). The model categorizes the features of a product into four components depending on a customer's provided Level of Functionality.

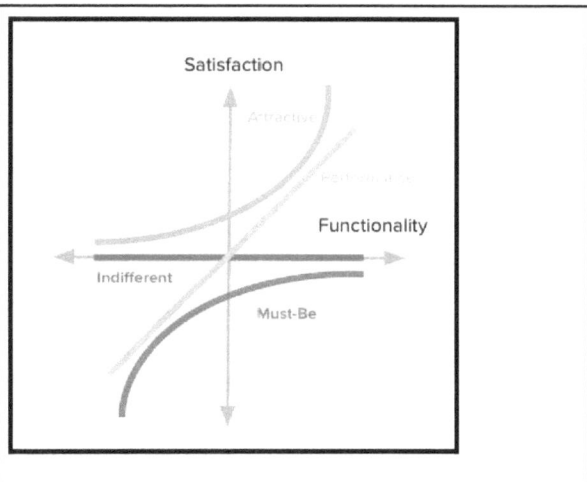

Figure 3. Graph of four categories of features

First is performance. As seen on the yellow line in the picture, the figure 3 is shown to be linear. This means that the more that the product is produced, the more satisfied the consumer will be. An example would be purchasing a car for its mileage attribute. As seen in the graph of figure 3 as well, every increase of functionality also increases the performance of the product. Second is the product being a "must-be". The features of the product should usually be what the customer expects from it. An example would be a mobile phone where the customer will expect that it can make calls and texts to other people. As seen in the figure 3's graphs, the must-be line is in a purplish color. It never reaches the positive part of the graph since a customer can never be fully satisfied with the functions of a product. No matter the amount of investment, a customer will always look for better options of the same product.

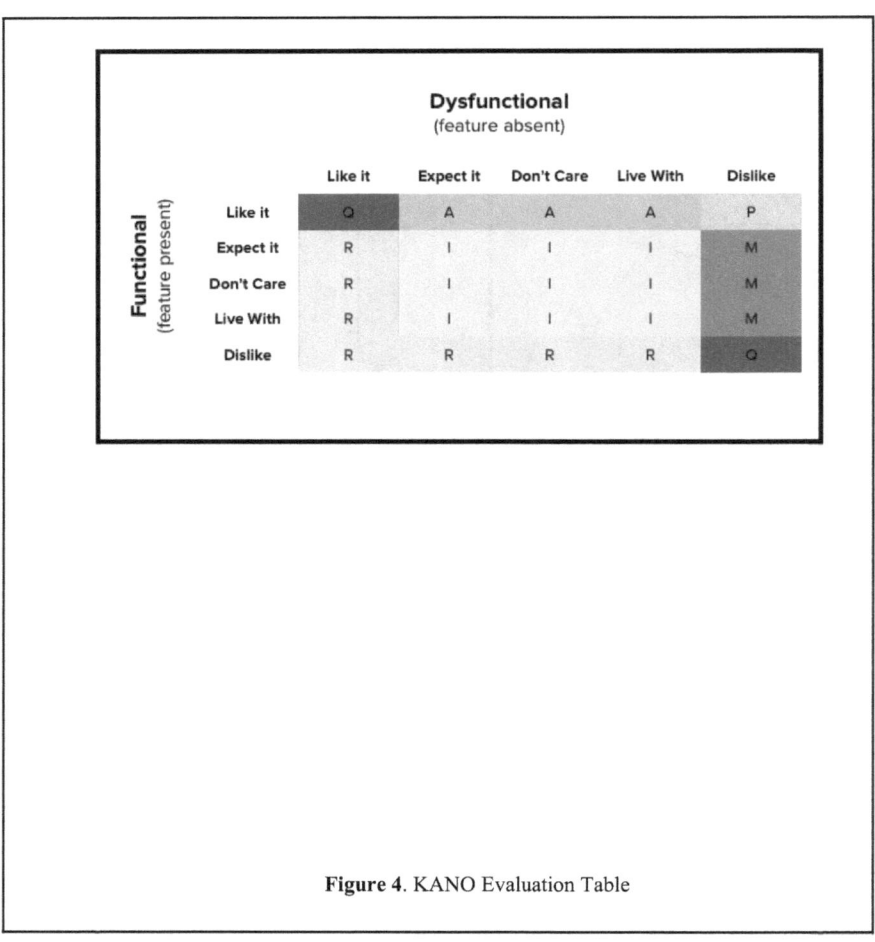

Figure 4. KANO Evaluation Table

Third is the attractiveness of a product. This attractiveness can be scaled into mild attractiveness to absolute delight. An example would be an iPhone where people are amazed at its many functions and its overall appearance which can appeal to a customer. In figure 4, attractiveness is represented by the blue line where it can range from being mildly attractive to mind-blowing attractiveness. Any point beyond that would be too much or "overkill".

Lastly is a product's indifference. This states that whether or not there is a presence of the product, there would be no significant difference to the surroundings of the customer. In figure 3, it is shown by a grey line. It connotes that it is rather not worth the investment because of its zero functionality and zero rise of satisfaction of a customer due to its constant form at zero (Zacarias, n.d.). It must be taken into account that the model is static and not dynamic. What could have put a person in awe with the iPhone's touch screen capabilities back in 2007 can be a basic expectation of the customers today (Zacarias, n.d.).

The KANO questionnaire has a question pair that uncovers a customer's perceptions. It usually includes pairs of questions asking whether or not a product had a certain feature. One question focuses on the functional properties of a product and in contrast, the other focuses on the dysfunctional aspect of the product. These are not open-ended questions due to the specific phrasing of the questions such as "how do you feel…" questions where they would usually be answered by either the customer's like or dislike of the product. From these questions, an evaluation table can be made (see figure 5).

From this table, it can be derived two new categories namely: the customer has not fully understood the question, or the customer proposes that the product is opposite of what he or she wants. From there, it is clear that a customer does not want a product when he or she answers that he or she likes the dysfunctional aspect while disliking the functional aspect of the product. This can suggest that the customer wants something reverse of that offered by the product. In the case of conflicting answers, these questions will be put under "questionable questions" (Zacarias, n.d.).

Conceptual Framework

Figure 5 shows how the research was divided into sections: railway transit systems, commuter's satisfaction, and commuting time. The study delved into the relationship between the following factors: the comparison among the railway transit systems in Metro Manila (LRT Line 1, LRT Line 2, MRT Line 3); the commuter's satisfaction with regards to the comfort of usage of the rail transit and the purpose of using the rail transit; and their commuting time. The researchers conducted a survey to find out how these factors interplay with one another.

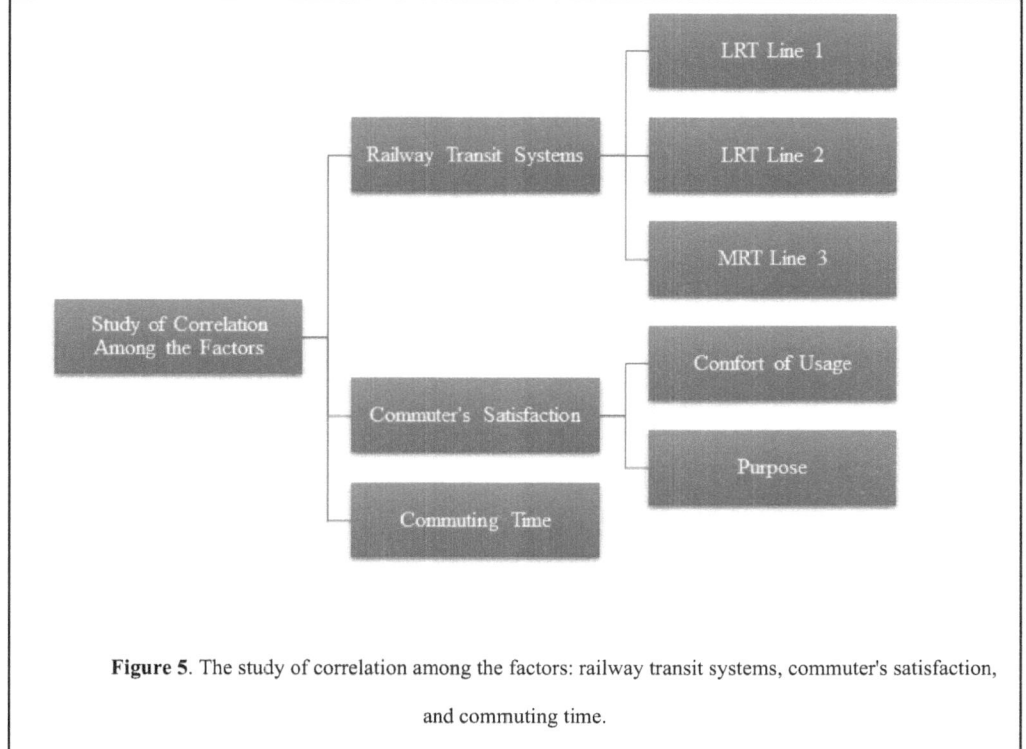

Figure 5. The study of correlation among the factors: railway transit systems, commuter's satisfaction, and commuting time.

To further discuss, the study determined how much of a difference there is in customer's satisfaction among the rail transit systems, whether LRT Line 1, LRT Line 2, or MRT Line 3 was the rail transit that offered the most satisfaction to their respective commuters. Their satisfaction came from their comfort in using the facilities of the rail transit system: a few examples would be their satisfaction with the number of chairs present in the train, their satisfaction with their experience of the air conditioning units in the train, so on and so forth. Another way to determine their satisfaction is by figuring out the purpose of why they take the rail transit systems: for example, if they were going to work and if they are consistently satisfied with the commuting time it takes them, if they were going to school and if they are also consistently satisfied with the commuting time, so on and so forth. And finally, the commuting time will take into account the moment they reach the station, how long they wait for the train, the approximate time of the journey they take inside the rail transit, and the approximate length of time it takes to leave the rail transit.

The researchers utilized the KANO model developed by Noriaki Kano to interpret the results taken from the survey. In the survey, the questions were based off of the discussion of factors above. The KANO model helped determine how satisfied the customers of the rail transit system are with the transport system that they are using. It further helped the researchers to discern the effectivity of the model, whether the rail transit systems satisfied the expectations of all the dimensions of the model or if they lack in certain areas. Thus, it helped pinpoint where the lack of satisfaction may come from using the rail transit system, allowing the researchers to concentrate and minimize the areas of problems and find ways to solve them.

Hypothesis

The basis was off the KANO model and the distributed survey. The satisfaction level of the consumer, the functionality level, the commuters' commuting time, and the perceived reliability of the service are the factors taken into consideration. As an effect, these factors are inversely proportional to the quality of the facilities of the train, depending on the railway transit system.

Definition of Terms

To further understand the contents of this research, the definitions of some key words or key terms as used in the research are as follows:

KANO Model. A theory for product development and customer satisfaction developed by Noriaki Kano back in 1984.

Reliability. The quality of being trustworthy or performing consistently well over time.

Railway Transit System. An all-encompassing term which refers to any type of local rail system that provides passenger service.

LRT Line 1. A rail transit line that runs from North Avenue to Baclaran.

LRT Line 2. A rail transit line that runs from Santolan to Recto.

MRT Line 3. A rail transit line that runs from North Avenue to Taft

Comfort of Usage. The amount of comfort that a consumer receives when utilizing a certain product or service

Satisfaction. Fulfillment of a need or a want.

Consumer. One who utilises economic goods; one who uses the rail transit system

Customer Satisfaction. The feeling of fulfilment that a consumer gets from the utilisation of an economic good

Commuting Time. In this research, the commuting time that will be accounted for will only be that on the train (Scope and Limitations).

Functionality. The quality or state of being able to perform the expected function

Dysfunction. Impaired or abnormal functioning within a whole system

Operational Framework

Customer Satisfaction. The researchers measured this variable by applying the KANO model into the survey questions. As previously stated in the Theoretical Framework, the KANO model is capable of determining what factors affect the overall experience of a commuter. It allows the researchers to segregate the components of the product (in this case, the train systems) and determine the reactions of the consumers to the quality of these components. Thus, the survey questions were written in such a way that each question provides information on the feelings of the correspondent to certain elements of their commuting experience. For example, the answers the researchers receive to the hypothetical question "How do you feel towards the presence of security guards around the entrances of the train stations" will determine if this is an element that is required, or simply preferred, or completely irrelevant, towards the experience of a commuter. By doing this, the researchers hope to isolate or identify key elements in the experience of a commuter that negatively affect the correspondent's experience and feelings toward the mode of transport.

Reliability. The researchers measured this variable by asking survey questions, again pertaining to how their experience is affected by specific factors. However, with regard to reliability, these questions specifically targeted tangible, real world repercussions of the current state of the train's reliability. The correspondents were asked to indicate how many times on average they experience delays or breakdowns while using the MRT or LRT systems. This allowed the researchers to quantify the perceived reliability of the MRT or LRT systems. They were then asked to answer open-ended questions that allowed the researchers to observe, not only the correspondent's perception of reliability, but also what repercussion the correspondent receives as a result of the reliability or unreliability of the train system and what factors commuters think contribute to the reliability/unreliability of the system. In determining the correspondent's perception of MRT/LRT reliability, as well as seeing the perceived repercussions of such reliability on their life after commuting, the researchers can narrow down what factors need urgent attention in order to improve service quality and reliability.

Commuting Time. The researchers looked at commuting time to see if there is a relationship between perceived quality of service and time spent commuting. For example, a correspondent may feel that their commuting time is lengthened and made more difficult as a result of poor quality services. Conversely, it is also possible that a correspondent may feel that their time spent commuting is not affected at all by reliability, or they may feel that it is irrelevant to change the time spent commuting. As a result, the researchers will ask the correspondent to input their average time spent commuting on a ratio scale, so as to ease the process of determining the median and mode of time spent commuting.

Synthesis

Based on the information above, the importance of the presence of train systems as a mode of transportation, especially in the context of the Philippines, cannot be understated. This fact further validates the reliance of Filipino commuters on the efficiency of the said mode of transportation, as the action of taking the train affects a person's stress levels. However, due to the historical context of its construction, particularly during the Spanish occupation, the efficiency of the various train systems was vastly and negatively affected. In addition to the context of its construction, a study by Shigeru Morichi and Tetsuo Shimizu (2006) cites the railway policies for developing countries are " in the vicious circle with low service level, lack of capacity, limited demand, politically decided fare, low efficiency of operation and lack of investment for infrastructure and rolling stock," all of which are applicable qualities for the railway systems in the Philippines. In contrast to the negativity of these statements, the Philippine government has strived to improve upon the lacking qualities, namely Empathy, Reliability, Responsiveness, Assurance, and Tangibility, which affect the service quality and customer satisfaction regarding the railway systems in the Philippines since presently in 2018, the LRTA have 5 projects for the LRT, 3 of which are locally funded and two foreign assisted in addition to the minor and major improvements done in the previous years.

Chapter 3

Methodology

The study was conducted to determine the commuter's satisfaction with commuting in the various types of railway transit systems in Metro Manila. The researchers used a quantitative method that focuses on the correlational approach. 45 participants were asked to answer the survey-questionnaire, which was the research instrument of the study. The results and interpretations of the answers were dependent on the statistical analyses that were held by the end of the data gathering period.

Research Design

The research has a quantitative paradigm and correlational approach. The nature of the research leads the design towards the quantitative paradigm. The quantitative aspect helps categorize the variables into independent, dependent, or controlled. This allows a completely unbiased point of view towards the data that will be gathered, unlike a qualitative research that delves into the emotional aspect of the data.

Choosing the correlational approach enables the exploration of the relationship between the variables using statistical analyses. Utilization of this method will lead to an observation-focused study, which is what the researchers will aim to record.

The method that was used for gathering data is the survey-questionnaire method, wherein the researchers asked the participants to answer questions regarding the topic by using a questionnaire. The answers were interpreted through the means of statistical analyses. The analyses helped keep the interpretations neutral and fair for the answers that will be received.

Variables and Measure

Railway Use. It is important to know which line the commuters are taking in order to segregate the responses efficiently and effectively. In the Philippines' railway transit system, different lines are managed by different authorities. The LRT lines are managed by the Light Rail Transit Authority (LRTA), while the MRT is managed by the Metro Rail Transit Corporation (MRTC). The quality of the lines is independent of each other, which means that the data collected on one line (e.g. the MRT Line 3) cannot be applied to analysis on the LRT train lines. In order to determine which line is being used, each participant will answer a question (on the nominal scale) that will indicate which line they are giving data for. The survey will ask "What train line are you being surveyed on?" with the only possible answers being:

1. LRT-1

2. LRT-2

3. MRT-3

Customer Satisfaction. As stated previously, customer satisfaction will be a variable that will help determine what factors would the commuters value and would like the line operators to improve on. For this variable, we will be using an ordinal scale in our questions. For example, in the aforementioned question, "How do you feel towards the presence of security guards around the entrances of the train stations," the question can be rated from scores 1 to 5. A score of 1 will be Very Unsatisfied, a score of 2 will be Unsatisfied, a score of 3 will be Neutral, a score of 4 will be Satisfied, and a score of 5 will be Very Satisfied. The questions will be categorized according to the different elements of the KANO model (Attractive, Performance, Indifferent, Must-Be, Reverse) and the final score will be calculated using the model to determine how the MRT stacks up in each of the categories.

Reliability. Reliability will be a variable that is measured on two different scales. The first scale will be a ratio scale, which asks the participant how frequently in a month they experience breakdowns, delays, or the like, while using the MRT or LRT lines. Sample answers for the sake of illustration will be "less than 4 times, 4 to 8 times, 8 to 12 times, 12 times or more," as the answers will change depending on data obtained prior to data gathering, on average breakdowns that occur in a month on the lines. The second part to interpreting reliability will involve, again, an ordinal scale, as the correspondents will be asked how much they feel the reliability of the lines affects their daily life. This allows the researchers to determine what factors urgently require attention.

Commuting Time. The researchers will ask the correspondent to input their average time spent commuting on a ratio scale. Primarily, this is because commuting time is best quantified on a ratio scale, given its lack of negative values. After all, time cannot be negative. The participants will then be asked to answer open ended questions on the ordinal scale, such as "how much do you feel commuting time affects productivity," or "how strongly do you wish that commuting time could be shortened."

Research Participants

The participants of the study consisted of commuters of the railway transit system in Metro Manila. The researchers were unable to obtain a quota of at least 60 participants, but have gathered 45 participants instead. The participants were mostly composed of people of the same age range, that is 15-20, who were mostly students as they were more likely to utilise the services of the trains frequently. The researchers administered the survey to the researchers' respective online friend lists, by doing a systematic random sampling to those who fit the criteria.

Sampling

The group applied a combination of two methods of sampling namely, Systematic Random Sampling and Purposive Sampling. Systematic Random Sampling was used since the selection of the participants did not affect the quality of the sample, provided that they are within the target demographic of commuters. Every two people were chatted in order to keep the sampling random. This ensures the randomness of the participants taking the survey. Furthermore, the use of Purposive Sampling in conjunction with the use of Systematic Random Sampling ensured that the participants were within the target demographic of commuters whilst ensuring that members within the population were given equal chances of being selected for the study.

Instruments

The research instrument that was primarily used was the Questionnaire, more particularly, a survey. This survey was specifically tailored to fit the KANO model. For example, some of the questions addressed particular aspects of the KANO such as performance and necessity. Moreover, the answers to the survey were quantified using the Semantic Differential Scale since this fit the KANO model due to the fact that the model itself relied on the feeling of the participants in relation to the product. The customer's satisfaction was measured in a Likert-Type scale of 1 to 5 which was based on the KANO model. The survey was created using Google Docs in order for the dissemination of the survey to be easier as only a link needs to be shared in order for a randomly selected individual to answer the survey.

The Chronbach's Alpha of the survey is at a mean of $\alpha=1.23$ which is an excellent rating for the survey. There is a mean of the Chronbach's Alpha due to the survey being divided into four components namely Time, Comfort, Reliability, and Security. The respective Chronbach's Alphas were respectively computed in excel using the formula shown in Figure 6.

$$\alpha = \frac{n}{n-1}\left(1 - \frac{\sum\limits_{i} V_i}{V_t}\right) \quad \text{(Cronbach, 1951, p. 299)}$$

Fig ure 6. Panayides, P. (2013, June 26). [Chronbach's Alpha Formula]. Retrieved March 11, 2019, from Panayides, P. (2013). Coefficient Alpha: Interpret With Caution. Retrieved March 11, 2019, from https://ejop.psychopen.eu/article/view/653/html

This was the reference used by the researchers in order to solve the Chronbach's alpha correctly with the use of Excel. The Chronbach's Alphas (rounded to 2 decimal places) of the survey are as follows where the Time component of the survey got a total of $\alpha = 1.11$ as shown in figure 7. Meanwhile, the alpha for the Comfort component is $\alpha = 1.10$ as shown in figure 8. Moving on, the alpha for the Reliability component of the survey is $\alpha = 1.12$ as shown in figure 9; the alpha for the Security component of the survey is at $\alpha = 1.49$ as shown in figure 10. To conclude, figure 11 shows the mean of all the Chronbach's alphas at $\alpha = 1.23$

Variance of Total score	295.4375
Sum of Item Variance	7.267489712
Chronbachs Alpha	1.114743912
(8 items)	

Figure 7. Chronbach's Alpha for Time component of the survey.

1.580246914	0.3155006859
60	38
Variance of Total score	358.8888889
Sum of Item Variance	8.995884774
Chronbachs Alpha	1.096800826
(9 Items)	

Figure 8. Chronbach's Alpha for the Comfort component of the survey.

1.283950617	0.2331961591	1
75	125	
Variance of Total	336.9375	
Sum of Item Vari:	8.087791495	
Chronbachs Alph	1.115424191	
(8 items)		

Figure 9. Chronbach's Alpha for the Reliability component of the survey.

0.8093278464	0.3895747599
106	119
Variance of Total score	468.2222222
Sum of Item Variance	2.263374486
Chronbachs Alpha	1.492749038
(3 items)	

Figure 10. Chronbach's Alpha for the Security compcnent of the survey

Chronbach's Alpha Mean	1.234991351

Figure 11. Survey's Chronbach's Alpha taken from the mean of all four components.

Procedures for Data Gathering

A small random sample from the participants was selected. The resulting questionnaire of the new survey created underwent pilot testing with this sample in order to see whether or not the survey was feasible and reliable for the study. The pilot testing was performed both online and physically in order to simulate the real conditions of the survey when taken physically. The feedback from the pilot tests, both physical ard online, were taken into consideration in order to further improve the survey. Upon the revisions, a full-blown survey was conducted online.

The online survey (Appendix A) was conducted through the use of Google Docs through the systematic random sampling done. The researchers browsed their friends lists where they counted every two people where the list was sorted in alphabetical order. The link was sent to the selected participant after confirming that he/she matched the target demographic set.

Using Google Docs made the data analysis more streamlined as the survey results went straight into Google's automatic analysis, where the researchers directly interpreted the findings. When the quota of at least 60 participants has been realized, data analysis for the results of the survey shall commence.

Procedures for Data Analysis

Coming from the data gathered above, the data was collated into a single uniform Excel sheet. From this excel sheet, the observed data from the KANO model was computed. The scoring for the model was distinct depending on what aspect of the model. Customer's satisfaction was measured in a scale of 1 to 5. The computed values of each aspect determined where the product (in this case, the train system) fell under in terms of functionality and how the customers see this product. Each finding was put on a table which compared the train lines' findings. The values were averaged and moved to the fourth excel page.

A second Excel page was dedicated to the ratio scale where it assigned a nominal number to each of the four categories where a score of 1 is assigned to "4 Times", a score of 2 is assigned to "4-8 Times", a score of 3 is assigned to "8-12 Times", and a score of 4 is assigned to "12 or more Times". The values were averaged and moved to the fourth excel page.

A third Excel page was made in order to view all the computed values that correspond to each train line side by side.

Chapter 4

Analysis and Interpretation of Data

At the conclusion of data gathering, a total of 45 respondents were able to answer the survey. Although this number is below the projected quota of at least 60 respondents, there are some notable results to some of the items in the questionnaire which shall be discussed in detail in the following chapter.

Results from Preliminary Questions

In figure 12, it is notable that the majority of respondents have most recently taken the LRT 2 train which runs from Recto until Santolan station. This is followed by the LRT 1 train from Baclaran to Roosevelt station and finally, the

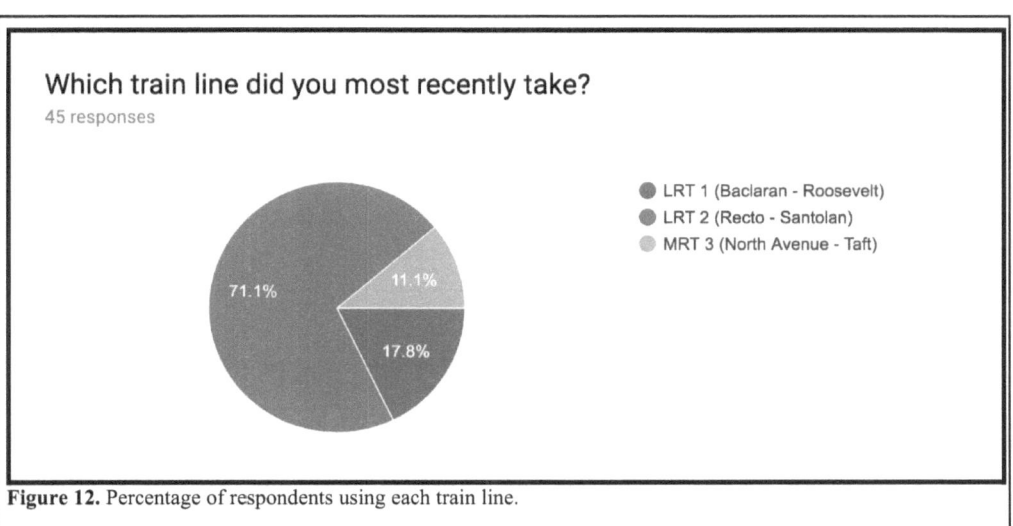

Figure 12. Percentage of respondents using each train line.

MRT 3 which runs from North Avenue up to Taft station. These percentages, namely the LRT 2 at 71.1% which is followed by the LRT 1 at 17.8% which is finally followed by the MRT 3 at 11.1%. From these results, the majority of which are from the LRT 2, cannot fully generalize the commuting population of the Train Lines in the Philippines.

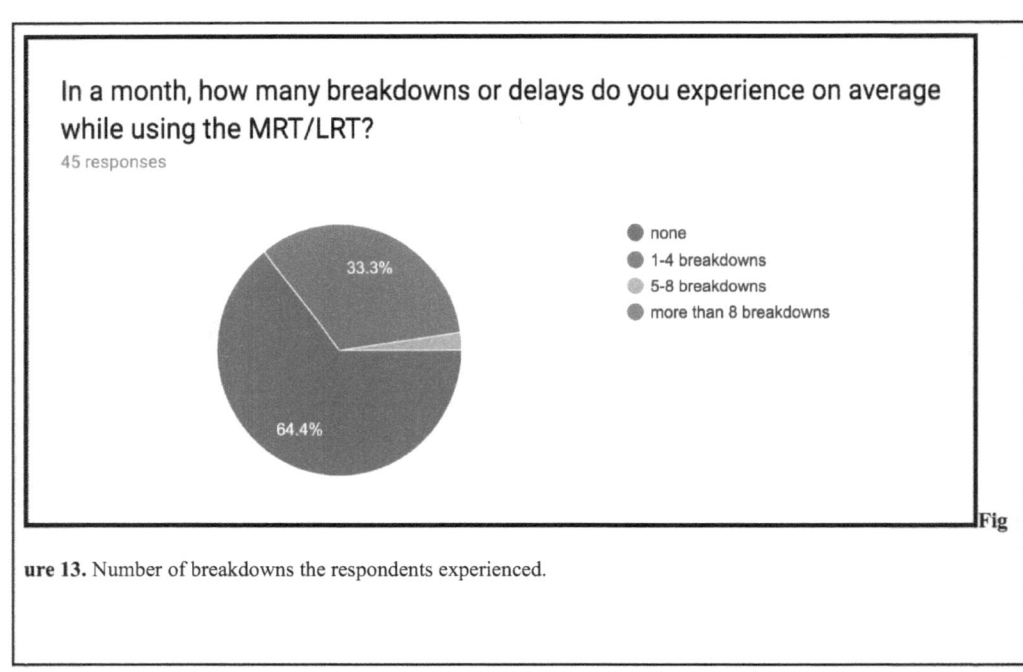

ure 13. Number of breakdowns the respondents experienced.

Although 64.4% of respondents answered that they have not experienced breakdowns and delays, 33.33% of the 45 respondents or simply, 15 respondents, answered that they have experienced an obstruction to the train's operation at least 1-4 times while a person who accounts for 2.2% of 45 respondents has experienced 5-8 times as shown in figure 13. This will have a definite effect on how this particular group of respondents, which account for a combined 35.53% of the 45 respondents may already have a dissatisfied viewpoint before they even begin answering the main KANO survey which is premised around getting the very satisfaction of the respondents.

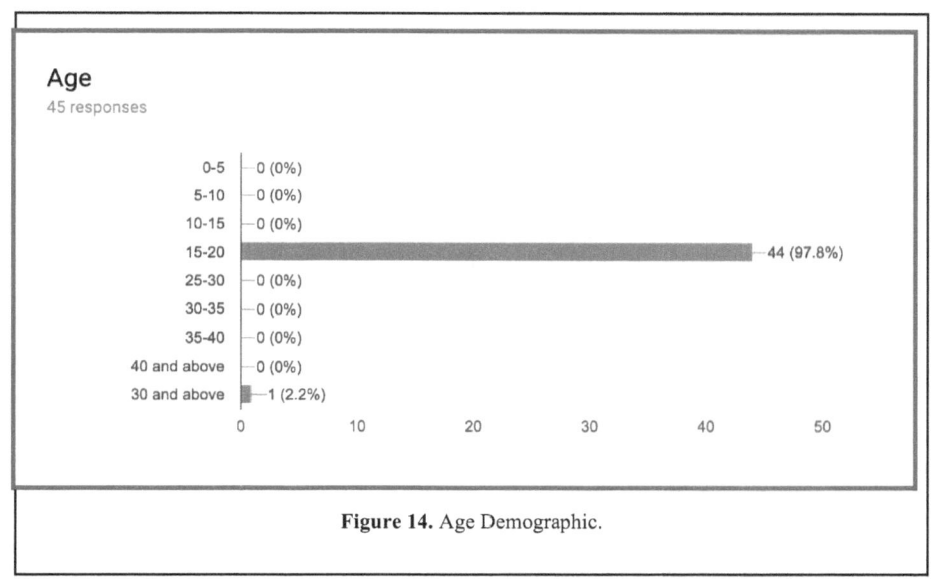

Figure 14. Age Demographic.

Results from Demographic Data

From the demographic results what is most noteworthy about the age demographic shown in Figure 14 shows that 44 out of the 45 participants (97.8%) are included in the age range of 15-20 while the remaining participant (2.2%) is included in the age range of 30 and above. Based on this, we can generalize that most of the participants are students who attend schools near one of the 11 stations that are part of the LRT 2 route. Moreover, it can be assumed that the participants experience rush hour during the time they commute, considering the fact that many other students, along with other demographics, commute using the LRT 2.

Results from the Main Questionnaire

From the 45 respondents, there are some notable items worth mentioning. A notable item would be the item that states "I would like it if my time spent commuting is lessened". A total of 28 people strongly agreed while 13 agreed. This then brings those who generally agree to a number of 41 which is roughly 91% of the total respondents which is 45. It can be concluded from this item that generally, people want to get to their final destinations as quickly as possible. In figure 15, the graph in the middle that shows all the data summarized by Google Docs as the survey was disseminated online through this medium. This will hold true for the next few notable results from the survey.

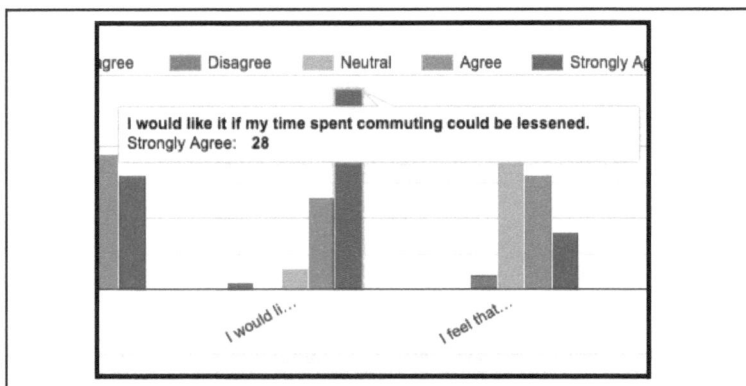

Figure 15. Result to the item that states "I would like it if my time spent commuting could be lessened".

Another item that is notable is a neutral item. As shown in figure 15, the ratio of those agreeing and disagreeing to this item is almost equal to the item, "I dislike taking the MRT/LRT because of how unreliable it can be". The indecisiveness could be due to many outside factors, but it can be generalized from this result that people have mixed emotions and feelings of the train systems on whether or not the systems are reliable respectively.

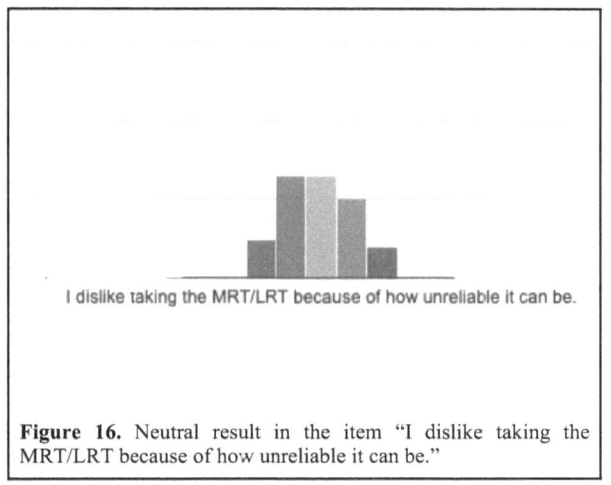

I dislike taking the MRT/LRT because of how unreliable it can be.

Figure 16. Neutral result in the item "I dislike taking the MRT/LRT because of how unreliable it can be."

The last notable item in the survey is a majorly agreeable statement in the questionnaire is the item "I would prefer it if the train had air-conditioning / the train's air-conditioning was working". As shown by the bar graph in figure 17, there are a total of 30 people who strongly agreed while 12 agreed to make a total of 42 out of the 45 people who felt that they agreed to this statement. These 42 people account for 93.33% of the total population which answered the survey. It can be generalized that while taking the train, people want to be comfortable, thus they want air-conditioning. The comfort of a customer has a lot to do with his satisfaction and, in conclusion, it can be extrapolated that people who are in hot carriages aboard the trains are generally not satisfied with the services or the lack thereof. This kind of result was same for questions related to the presence of Wi-Fi signal within the stations and the trains. This means that the convenience of having Wi-Fi signal and air-conditioning within the trains and the stations greatly increases the satisfaction of the customers using the trains.

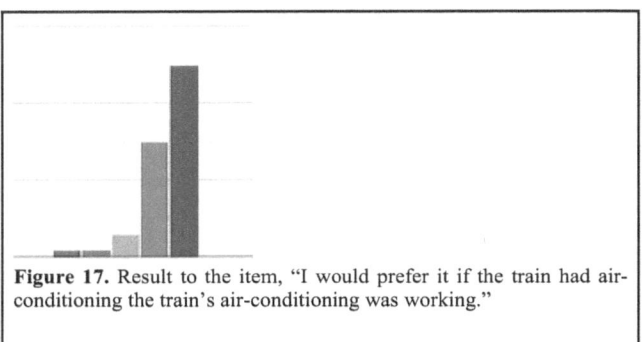

Figure 17. Result to the item, "I would prefer it if the train had air-conditioning the train's air-conditioning was working."

Survey Anova results

A one-way anova test was done and the results are as follows. The survey was split into four factors namely Time, Comfort, Reliability, and Security, which made up the survey questionnaire. As a result, there were separate anova tests done for each survey part which were then combined and computed for their mean in order to determine the overall significance of the survey.

Analyzing the Significance of the train line to the train line. When analyzing all the items respectively for any significant findings through the anova test to find the significance of the train line on the passenger's satisfaction, there were none found as all the items had alphas that were above $\alpha= 0.05$. The lowest α to 0.05 was the item, "I feel that the trains on the MRT/LRT are too slow.", where it had an alpha of 0.113 as seen in figure 18.

VAR00003	Between Groups	2.800	2	1.400	2.363	.113
	Within Groups	16.000	27	.593		
	Total	18.800	29			

Figure 18. Anova result of individual item "I feel that the trains on the MRT or LRT are too slow.

When comparing the results of each item, it can be seen that none of the items are equal or below the $\alpha= 0.05$ mark. The lowest alpha level was stated above at 0.113 which is still above the 0.05 threshold of the Anova tested.

The whole survey was then tested, and the results are shown in figure 19.

ANOVA

		Sum of Squares	df	Mean Square	F	Sig.
Security	Between Groups	.453	2	.226	1.007	.379
	Within Groups	6.069	27	.225		
	Total	6.522	29			
Reliability	Between Groups	.389	2	.195	1.074	.356
	Within Groups	4.890	27	.181		
	Total	5.279	29			
Comfort	Between Groups	.019	2	.009	.081	.922
	Within Groups	3.158	27	.117		
	Total	3.177	29			
Time	Between Groups	.130	2	.065	.416	.664
	Within Groups	4.206	27	.156		
	Total	4.335	29			

Figure 19. Anova Result of the whole survey for the significance of the train line on the satisfaction of the customer.

It can be seen that none of the values have a significance below 0.05. The mean of the survey's significance is $\alpha= 0.57525$.

Analyzing the Significance of the commuting time on the customers' satisfaction. The results are generally the same for this one wherein all the items do not go below the 0.05

significance level. There were no items notable for further discussion in this part of the survey. The overall survey significance per part is shown in figure 20.

ANOVA

		Sum of Squares	df	Mean Square	F	Sig.
Time	Between Groups	.791	2	.396	3.013	.066
	Within Groups	3.544	27	.131		
	Total	4.335	29			
Comfort	Between Groups	.594	2	.297	3.103	.061
	Within Groups	2.584	27	.096		
	Total	3.177	29			
Reliability	Between Groups	.230	2	.115	.614	.548
	Within Groups	5.049	27	.187		
	Total	5.279	29			
Security	Between Groups	.449	2	.224	.998	.382
	Within Groups	6.073	27	.225		
	Total	6.522	29			

Figure 20. Anova Result of the whole survey for the significance of the commuting time on the satisfaction of the customer.

This is the closest result to the significance of 0.05 where the comfort section of the survey missed this by 0.011. Nonetheless, the mean of the survey for this variable is $\alpha= 0.26425$ which is also higher than the significance level needed to have a type I error. In result, a type II error was committed.

Chapter 5

Summary, Conclusions, and Recommendations

The following chapter concludes the study, where the research is summarized, and the findings of the study is discussed. The objective of the study is to compare the rail transit systems that are located in Metro Manila in terms of its respective commuters' perceptions regarding the length of their commuting time and their satisfaction with the facilities of the transit systems. All the objectives laid out in chapter one have been fulfilled, which are to be discussed further.

For the literature review, the history of the rail transit systems was discussed in the context of the Philippines. The researchers also tackled international rail transit systems, as well as other common modes of transportation, to provide more context to why Filipinos are using rail transit systems even with a lot of choices for transportation to choose from. It boiled down to the fact that rail transit systems held a standard for its facilities, which the Philippines modeled after other international rail transit systems, which other modes of transportation did not live up to.

For methodology, all of the data gathering and analysis were done through online means, specifically through Google Docs, Microsoft Excel, and SPSS. This meant for easier data collection as Google had automatic preliminary analysis.

For interpretation of data, the results from the one-way anova tests have yielded to no significant difference. However, the results from the survey have concluded that the commuters are not generally satisfied with the facilities of the rail transit systems and want more improvements with that aspect. Therefore, a type II error is present, which is the failure to reject a false null hypothesis.

Findings

Notable results from the survey were presented. People generally want to get to their destinations faster. This is because most of the participants are from the age range 15-20. This means that they are most likely students, thus, the need to get to their destination faster stems from the fact that, possibly, they do not want to be late for school. People have expressed neutrality in terms of the reliability of the rail transit systems. It is split evenly between agree and disagree, thus, other factors are involved in why the participants have mixed reactions towards the reliability. These factors were not within the scope of our data gathering. People also want to improve on the facilities, specifically on the air-conditioning units of the trains. Because their satisfaction comes from the comfort of usage with the facilities, they agreed that they want the air-conditioning units to be better or to simply start working, so that these commuters will be comfortable during their commute in the rail transit system.

From the results in the one-way Anova testing, several results were found. The comparison from each train line to train line bore no significant difference. This meant among all the train lines, the overall commuters' satisfaction was generally the same. The findings regarding commuting time also bore no significant difference. This meant that no matter how much the length of commuting time varied between one commuter to another, it generally meant that it did not make a huge difference with each commuter's satisfaction.

Conclusions

Referring back to the research questions, a lot of the commuters that partook in this study are from the age range 15-20, thus, it is concluded that the study's participants are students.

Referring back to the research objectives, there was no significant difference in the satisfaction among the respective commuters of LRT 1, LRT 2, and MRT 3. The commuters would like the facilities in the rail transit systems, like the air-conditioning units, to improve to have better satisfaction with using these trains. The researchers could not quantify which rail transit system provides the least satisfaction because there was no significant difference in the satisfaction of the commuters of these lines.

The researchers believe that the Filipino commuters, the Philippine government, and specific academic institutions like University of Santo Tomas, San Beda University, Arellano University and Far Eastern University Manila could benefit from this research. Filipino commuters take the rail transit systems and can benefit from knowing how the facilities can decrease their satisfaction with this choice of transportation. The Philippine government can benefit from knowing how much more they can improve on the rail transit systems. The institutions can benefit from knowing how much of their student population take the rail transit systems, eliminating a lot of traffic from those who take private transportation in going to school.

Recommendations

For future research, the researchers would recommend expanding the number of participants to a much larger scale, particularly in the four-digit number. This is because the more participants that can input data for the study, then the more generalizations can be found among all three lines. Because of time constraints, the researchers were not able to gather a more concrete result to the reason why there was no significant difference in the satisfaction levels among the three rail transit systems. Having more participants will help signify that difference.

The researchers also recommend expanding the participants in terms of age range. This is because the needs of a student can differ from the needs of a worker, of a senior citizen, and so on. This will help provide more context as to how their satisfaction needs can be met as well as more diversity to the sample at hand.

Appendix

Survey used for data gathering.

Good afternoon! We are researchers from Ateneo de Manila Senior High writing a topic on Customer's Satisfaction on Train Lines in Metro Manila. We hope to gather your input to further help our research. Thank you for your valuable time!

Section 1: Please tick the letter that corresponds best to your answer. This section is about your general experience with the rail transit system in Metro Manila.

1. Please indicate (encircle the letter of) the train line you are being surveyed about.

a.   LRT-1 (Baclaran - Roosevelt)

b.   LRT-2 (Recto - Santolan)

c.   MRT-3 (North Avenue - Taft)

2. On average, how much time do you spend commuting within a day?

a.   Less than 1 hour

b.   1 to 2 hours

c.   2 to 3 hours

d.   More than 3 hours

3. In a day, on average, how much time do you spend commuting using the MRT or LRT?

a.   Less than 30 minutes

b.   30 minutes to 1 hour

c.   1 hour to 1 hour and 30 minutes

d.   More than 1 hour and 30 minutes

Section 2: Please choose the number that corresponds best to your answer. This section is about your experience with the rail transit system when it comes to the length of commuting time.

KANO Model

Statement	Strongly Disagree	Disagree	Neutral	Agree	Strongly Agree
4. Commuting time affects the amount of time I am able to spend working.	1	2	3	4	5

5. I would like it if my time spent commuting could be lessened.	1	2	3	4	5
6. I feel that the trains on the MRT or LRT are too slow.	1	2	3	4	5
7. When I am late, it is **most likely** because the MRT or LRT was also late.	1	2	3	4	5
8. The amount of time I spend at work is **NOT** affected by the quality of service the MRT or LRT provides.	1	2	3	4	5
Statement	None at all.	1-4	5-8	More than 8.	Can't remember.

9. On average in a month, how many breakdowns or delays do you experience while using the MRT/LRT?	1	2	3	4	5

Section 3: Please encircle the number that corresponds best to your answer. This section is about statements that gauge your opinions regarding the comfort and satisfaction with usage of the rail transit systems.

Statement	Strongly Disagree	Disagree	Neutral	Agree	Strongly Agree
10. The MRT/LRT does not need anything important to be fixed.	1	2	3	4	5
11. If there were an alternative, I would not take the MRT/LRT at all.	1	2	3	4	5

12. When I take the MRT/LRT, I constantly worry that it will break down.	1	2	3	4	5
13. I often see security guards keeping the station secure.	1	2	3	4	5
14. I feel safe while taking the MRT/LRT.	1	2	3	4	5
15. The way the security is handled at the MRT/LRT station does not need to be improved.	1	2	3	4	5
16. Obtaining a ticket and boarding a train is not difficult.	1	2	3	4	5
17. While on a train, I feel comfortable.	1	2	3	4	5

18. I would prefer it if the train had air-conditioning / The train's air-conditioning was working.	1	2	3	4	5
19. I find that there is enough space for me and my belongings while on a train.	1	2	3	4	5
20. I find myself constantly wishing for more space while on a train.	1	2	3	4	5
21. The lack of free internet connection while inside the train station hinders the experience.	1	2	3	4	5
22. I would prefer it if there was internet connection while inside the train station.	1	2	3	4	5

	1	2	3	4	5
23. The introduction of the Beep card / Stored value card has made commuting easier.	1	2	3	4	5
24. The introduction of single use tickets has made commuting easier.	1	2	3	4	5
25. The lack of train schedules hinders my experience in commuting.	1	2	3	4	5
26. I would prefer it if trains had a set schedule.	1	2	3	4	5
27. I would prefer it if trains followed their schedule, if there is one.	1	2	3	4	5
28. Whether or not the train is late does not affect my commuting experience.	1	2	3	4	5

We thank you for your input and your time for answering this survey! For more inquiries, please email mikka.alexis@icloud.com.

References

Bueza, Michael. 2018. *MRT woes: How often do they happen?* Rappler. Retrieved November 23, 2018 from https://www.rappler.com/newsbreak/iq/188912-mrt-problems-frequency-data

Cantwell, M., Caulfield, B., & O'Mahony, M. (2009). Examining the Factors that Impact Public Transport Commuting Satisfaction. *Journal of Public Transportation*, *12* (2): 1-21. DOI: http://doi.org/10.5038/2375-0901.12.2.1.

Chandra Saha J. Public utility characteristics of railways in India. *IJRARE*. 2018; 5 (1) URL: http://ijrare.iust.ac.ir/article-1-180-en.html

DOTC. *About page*. Retrieved November 23, 2018, from https://dotcmrt3.gov.ph/about

Falzon, Edward, et al. 2017. *Where are the world's best metro systems?* CNN. Retrieved November 23, 2018, from

https://edition.cnn.com/travel/article/world-best-metro-systems/index.html.

Farajpour A, Bazeghi kisomi P, Bagheri M. Identifying the Factors Affecting on Service Quality & Passenger Satisfaction in Commuter Train Services. *IJRARE*. 2017; 4 (2) :57-66 URL: http://ijrare.iust.ac.ir/article-1-174-en.html

Higgins, C., Ferguson, M., & Kanaroglou, P. (2014). Light rail and land use change: Rail transit's role in reshaping and revitalizing cities. *Journal of Public Transportation*, *17*(2), 5.

Hunter-Zaworski, K. (2018). Modeling and Validation of Standards for a Sleeping

 Compartment on Accessible Passenger Rail Vehicles (No. Rail Safety IDEA Project

 31).

LRTA. (n.d.). LRTA History. Retrieved December 9, 2018, from

 http://www.lrta.gov.ph/index.php/history

LRTA. (2018, August 31). Project Status as of 2018. Retrieved December 9, 2018, from

 http://lrta.gov.ph/images/upload/project-status-as-of-august-31-2018.pdf

Mito, Yuko. *Corporate culture as strong diving force for punctuality- another "just in time".*

 Hitachi-Rail. Retrieved November 23, 2018, from

 https://web.archive.org/web/20081221165154/http://www.hitachi-

 rail.com/rail_now/column/just_in_time/index.html.

Morichi, S., & Tetsuo, S. (2006). A comparative study on recent railway development and

 operation policies in developed countries.

Norley, K. (2010). Light rail: the semi-metro concept. Paper delivered at the 33rd

 Australasian Transport Research Forum Conference held in Canberra, on 29

 September - 1 October 2010.

Orellana, Faye. 2018. *MRT-3 management says sorry over incident with PWD passenger.*

 Inquirer. Retrieved November 23, 2018, from

 https://newsinfo.inquirer.net/1050547/mrt-3-management-says-sorry-over-incident-wi

 th-pwd-passenger.

Orosa, R. L. (2013, July 19). Timeline: LRT, MRT construction. Retrieved December 9,

    2018, from

https://www.philstar.com/headlines/2013/07/19/987621/timeline-lrt-mrt-constructio

Palacin, Roberto. 2018. *Railway passenger satisfaction: how good is good?* Womble Bond

    Dickinson. Retrieved November 23, 2018, from

    https://www.womblebonddickinson.com/sites/default/files/2018-02/Railway

    passenger satisfaction.pdf.

Panayides, P. (2013). Coefficient Alpha: Interpret With Caution. Retrieved March 11, 2019,

    from https://ejop.psychopen.eu/article/view/653/html

Ramirez, Robertzon. 2018. *Trans woman complains of discrimination at MRT-3.* Philippine

    Star. Retrieved November 23, 2018, from

    https://www.philstar.com/nation/2018/09/12/1850675/trans-woman-complains-discri

    mination-mrt-3.

Rey, Aika. 2018. *After train breakdown, LRT 1 passengers walk along rail tracks.* Rappler.

    Retrieved November 23, 2018, from

    https://www.rappler.com/nation/214082-passengers-walk-along-lrt1-rail-tracks-octob

    er-11-2018.

Saif, M., maghrour zefreh, M., & Torok, A. (2018). Public transport accessibility: a

    literature review. *Periodica Polytechnica Transportation Engineering.* 3.

    10.3311/PPtr.12072.

Schmöcker, Jan-Dirk & Bell, Michael & Lam, William. (2004). *Special issue: Importance of public transport.* Journal of Advanced Transportation. 38. 1 - 4. 10.1002/atr.5670380102.

V. Profillidis. Challenges and Prospects of European Railways. *IJRARE*. 2014; 1 (1) :1-10

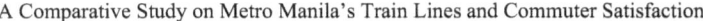

URL: http://ijrare.iust.ac.ir/article-1-46-en.html

Railway in Sweden and Japan – a comparative study. Trafikanalys. 2014.

Zacarias, D. (n.d.). The Complete Guide to the Kano Model. Retrieved from

https://foldingburritos.com/kano-model/

Curriculum Vitae

Mikka Alexis Mendoza

Contact Information

Name: Mikka Alexis T. Mendoza

Telephone: 621-2138

Cellphone: 09173202142

Email: mikkaalexis.mendoza@alumni.ateneo.edu

Education

Ateneo Grade School

Graduated 2014

Ateneo Junior High School

Graduated 2017

Employment History

Basketball Scorer and Timekeeper

2013

Bracken

Video Editor

December 2018

Computer Skills

C# programming

Basic HTML

Proficient in Final Cut pro

Basic skills in Adobe Premiere Pro

Awards

Outstanding Basketball Player Award

Coach E Basketball camp

2014

Philippine Athletic Youth Association (PAYA) Volleyball Tournament Champion

Midgets Division

2015

Held at Xavier University

St. Stanislaus Kostka Deportment Award

1st term

2017

Ateneo Junior High School

St. Jean de Brebeuf Award for Athletes

2018

Ateneo Junior High School

3rd Honors Award

1st Semester

2018

Ateneo Senior High School

Musical Background

Vox Angeli Children's Choir

2012-2013

Hail Mary the Queen Children's Choir

2013

Athletic Background

Ateneo Football Varsity Team (2009-2013)

Team Captain 2013-2014

Ateneo Track and Field Varsity (2013-2016)

Team Captain 2015-2016

Ateneo Midgets and Aspirants Volleyball Team (2014-2016)

Team Captain of Midgets 2015-2016

Ateneo High School UAAP Team (2016-2019)

Curriculum Vitae

Janelle Torres

Contact Information

Name: Janelle Fiona M. Torres

Telephone: 682-2970

Cell Phone: 09154040068

Email: janelle.torres07@gmail.com

Education

High School

- Ateneo de Manila Senior High School (year 2018-2019; present)

- St. Bridget School, Quezon City (years 2007-2018)

Employment History

Work History

- Student Videographer (years 2015-present)

- Student Photographer (years 2015-2018)

- Student Teacher (year 2017-2018)

Computer Skills

- Proficient in MS Word

- Proficient in MS PowerPoint

- Proficient in Vegas Pro 14

- Proficient in Wondershare Filmora

- Basic in Adobe Photoshop

Awards

Honorable Mention

- Years 2014-2018

- St. Bridget School, Quezon City

- SBS Administration

Second Honor

- Years 2014-2018

- St. Bridget School, Quezon City

- SBS Administration

First Honor

- Year 2015-2016
- St. Bridget School, Quezon City
- SBS Administration

With Honors

- Year 2017-2018
- St. Bridget School, Quezon City
- SBS Administration

Best in Filipino

- Years 2016-2018
- St. Bridget School, Quezon City
- SBS Administration

Best in English

- Years 2013-2018
- St. Bridget School, Quezon City
- SBS Administration

Professional Memberships

Lakambini committee

- · Member

- · Year 2018-2019

Frisbee organization

- · Member

- · Year 2018-2019

Sanggunian Communications Team

- · Writer

- · Year 2018-2019

Interests

- · Videography

- · Filmmaking

- · Creative writing

- · Nonfiction writing

- · Reading

- · English tutoring

- · Biking

- · Journalism

Curriculum Vitae

Luis Amatong

Contact Information

Name: Luis Andres Augusto P. Amatong

Contact Number: 09276489394

Email: luis_andres_augusto@yahoo.com

Education

Ateneo Grade School

Graduated 2014

Ateneo Junior High School

Graduated 2017

Ateneo Senior High School

(2018 - present)

Awards

National Semi-Finalist, Philippine Schools Debate Championship 2019

8th Best Speaker and Semi-Finalist, Inter-Secondary School Political Science Debate Cup 2018

School Top Scholar, World Scholar's Cup: Vietnam Round 2017

Octofinalist, Fast Forward 2018

Quarterfinalist, IDeA 2 2017

Quarterfinalist, Adelante Cup 2019

Champion Scholar, World Scholar's Cup, Manila Round 2018

3rd Place, SPCP Fair 2019: Retrospect

Pre-Quarterfinalist, Rotary National Debate Championship (RNDC) 2017

Quarterfinalist, IDeA Grands 2017

Interests

Guitar and Bass

Singing

Debating

Economics

Political Science

Infrastructure and Urban Planning

Curriculum Vitae

Denise Bayucan

Contact Information

Name: Marianne Denise J. Bayucan

Address: Cullallabo Del Sur, Burgos, Isabela, Philippines

Contact Number: +63 09176343051

Email: denliwaine@gmail.com

Education

High School: Philippine Yuh Chiau School

Senior High School: Ateneo De Manila University

Awards

International Competitions and Assessment for Schools English Credit

2011

Bendemeer Primary School

International Competitions and Assessment for Schools Science Distinction

2016

Philippine Yuh Chiau School

International Competitions and Assessment for Schools English Credit

2016

Philippine Yuh Chiau School

Curriculum Vitae

Marco Francisco

Contact Information

Name: Marco Angelo G. Francisco

Address: 23 T. Claudio Street, Morong, Rizal, Philippines

Contact Number: +639275709799

Email: mfrancisco0102@yahoo.com

Education

Primary School: Saint Jerome's Academy

Junior High School: Ateneo de Manila Junior High School

Senior High School: Ateneo de Manila Senior High School

Awards

First Honors Grades 1-3

Second Honors Grades 4-5

Third Honors Grade 6

Third Honors 3rd term Grade 7

Third Honors 2nd term Grade 8

Second Honors 2nd term Grade 9

Second Honors 1st term Grade 10